SHE

... A tribute to a woman I Love

Madhuri Joshi

INDIA • SINGAPORE • MALAYSIA

ISBN 979-8-89026-655-2

Dedicated To

Her

PREFACE

SHE is no less than a superhero. She is a force of nature. Her life itself is a big celebration. This tiny booklet is an ode to her truly magnificent life.

As she turns 60 this year, here are 60 reminiscences of a woman I absolutely love and adore and call, my MOM!

ABOUT HER

Dr.Uma Sudhakar is a consultant Obstetrician, Gynecologist and a Laparoscopic Surgeon from Bellary. She is married to an Ophthalmologist. They are blessed with two children who are both doctors and are married to doctors. She is a dynamic lady with various interests in other fields.

1

SHE is a woman of spirit. Shines bright. Gives light.

2

SHE is a powerhouse of energy, enthusiasm, and efficiency.

3

SHE is an absolute go-getter. Can't stop, won't stop.

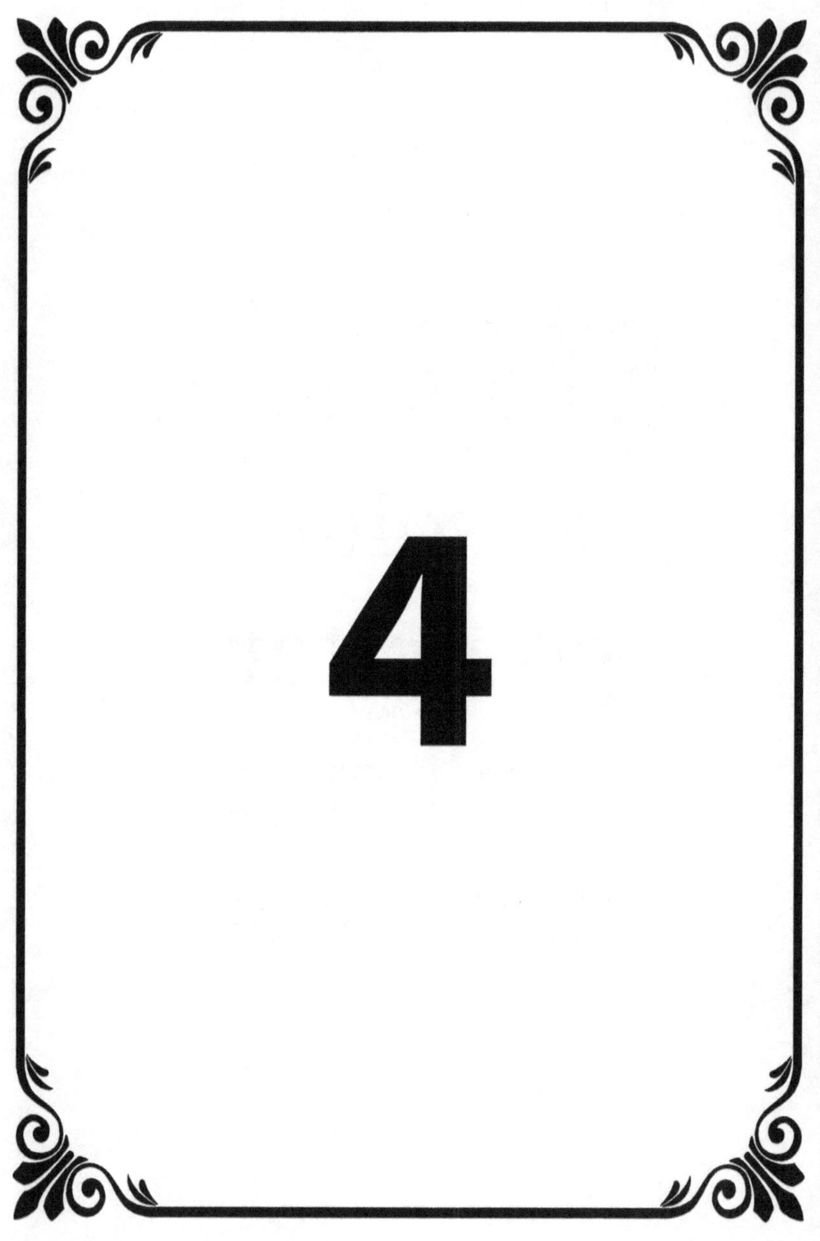

4

SHE is that woman who buys her own diamonds. And some paddy fields and mango farms too.

SHE feels daughters are the pillars of the house and daughters-in-law are its light. And she is a living example of both.

6

SHE

makes her children the center of her big world.

7

SHE makes the best freshly brewed filter coffee served in steel cup and saucer early in the morning. *Banna, ruchi, shakthi*-just perfect.

8

SHE is one of the best host one can ever have.

9

SHE has a husband who is so calm, to balance out her storm.

10

SHE has got all the eight *avatars* of Goddess Lakshmi.

11

SHE is an Ogcian magician... handles her profession so effortlessly.

12

SHE can cook a full course *bale ele* meal in a jiffy, served with dollops of love.

13

SHE has an exclusive saree showroom at home, with sarees of all colours and textures.

14

SHE had a lively childhood with her four siblings, as lively as her.

15

SHE has mastered the art of singing, another jewel in her crown.

16

SHE has *amruthaphala* in her hands. No wonder when she feeds, it tastes like heaven.

17

SHE is
a perfect example of a multitasker... can do a hundred things at the same time.

18

SHE

imitates people
so well that even
a mimicry artist
can get inspired.

19

SHE is *ammamma* to my daughter. In true sense of the word.

20

SHE has ventured into unchartered territories like a pro. And was of course successful.

21

SHE

had two
prerequisites for
my bridegroom.
I liked him,
she liked him.
And the rest is
history.

22

SHE is my biggest cheerleader and best critic.

23

SHE is so pious that her prayers can make *Shiva* come alive.

24

SHE

can travel
a thousand
kilometers
just for you,
anytime,
anywhere.

25

SHE is
a lady don
when it comes
to handling
her various
businesses.

26

SHE
is always 'present' for her kith and kin.

27

SHE leads
by example to
all her staff.
Work and
otherwise.

28

SHE hits it out of the park when it comes to event management.

29

SHE is the biggest admirer of doctor's profession, so much so that she made sure all her four children are doctors.

30

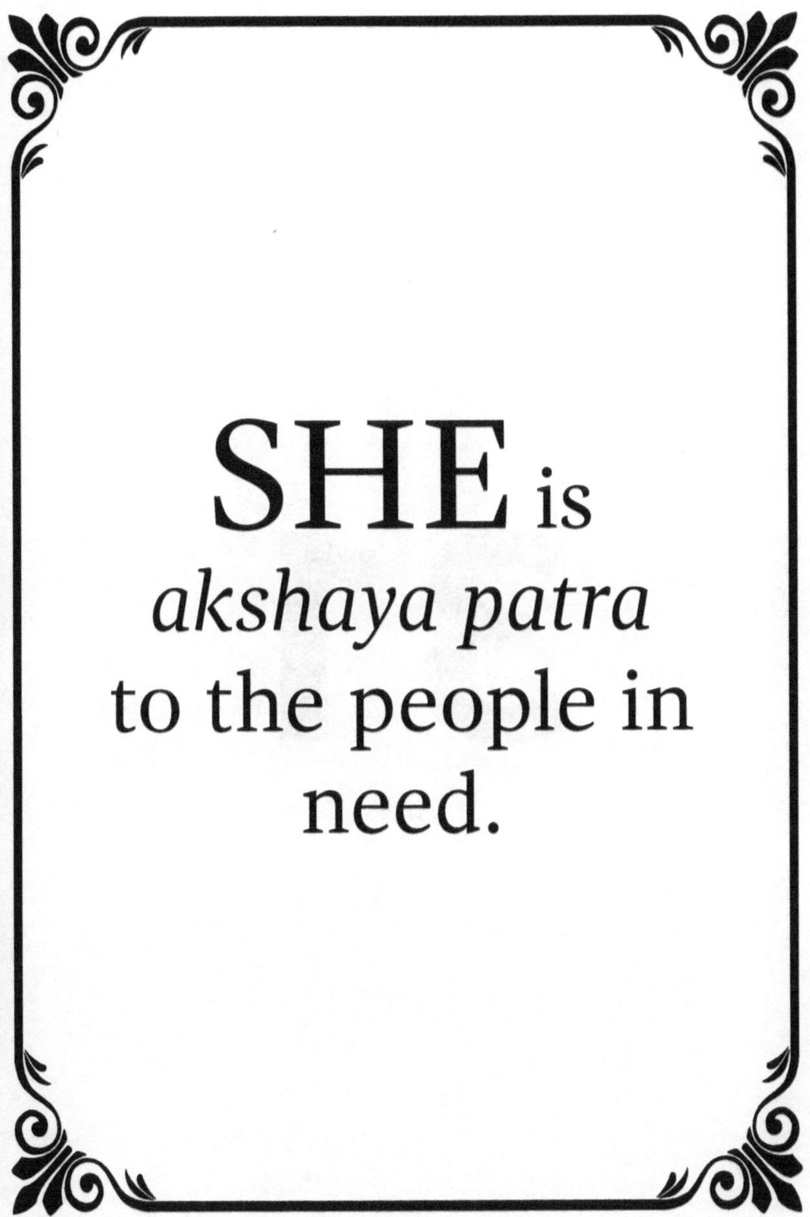

SHE is
akshaya patra
to the people in
need.

31

SHE has the talent of converting a piece of scrap into something exquisite.

32

SHE is like a sun, and all of us follow her direction for sunshine in our lives.

33

SHE

maintains her crew with equal amounts of love and strictness. Actually more love I would say.

34

SHE gives the right advice at the right time to set things right.

35

SHE is like a magnet who holds the pieces of extended family together.

SHE can make other people so comfortable that they can confide anything with her.

37

SHE
balances her personal and professional life beautifully.

38

SHE waters relationships with so much love and warmth, that they just bloom.

39

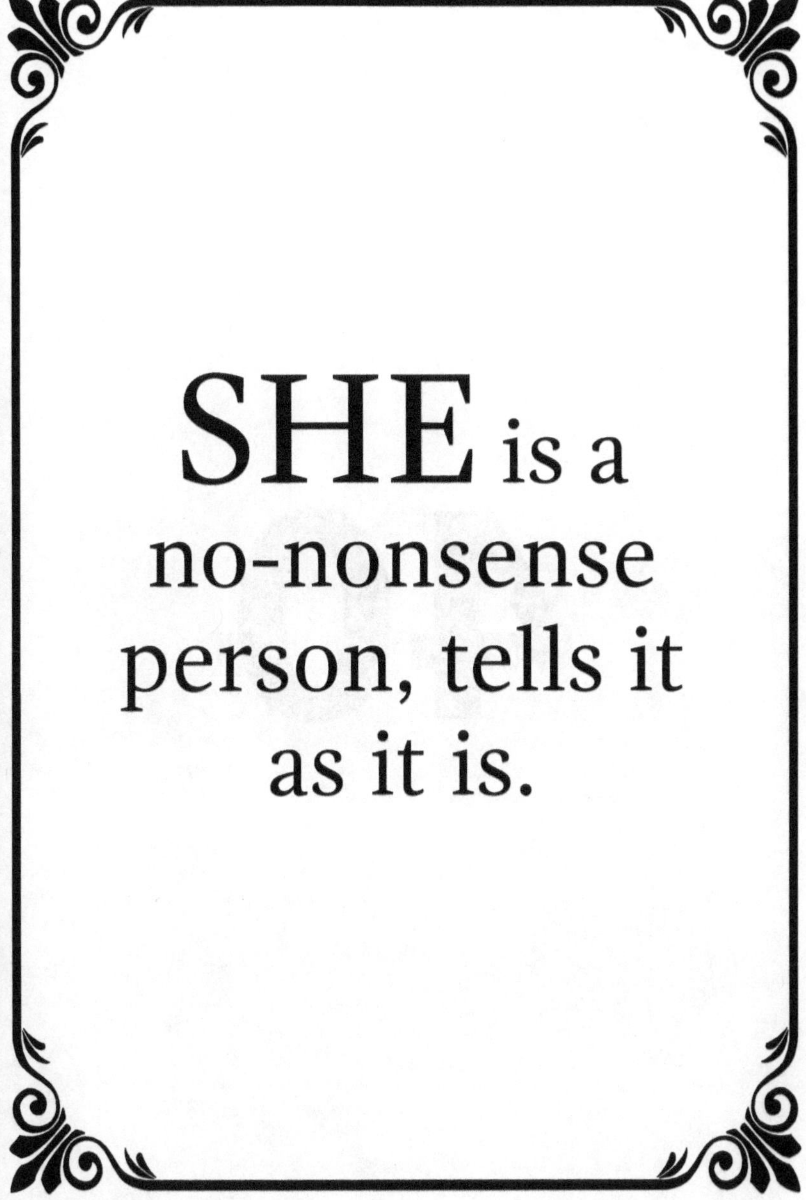

SHE is a no-nonsense person, tells it as it is.

SHE tells these funny anecdotes, very very funnily.

41

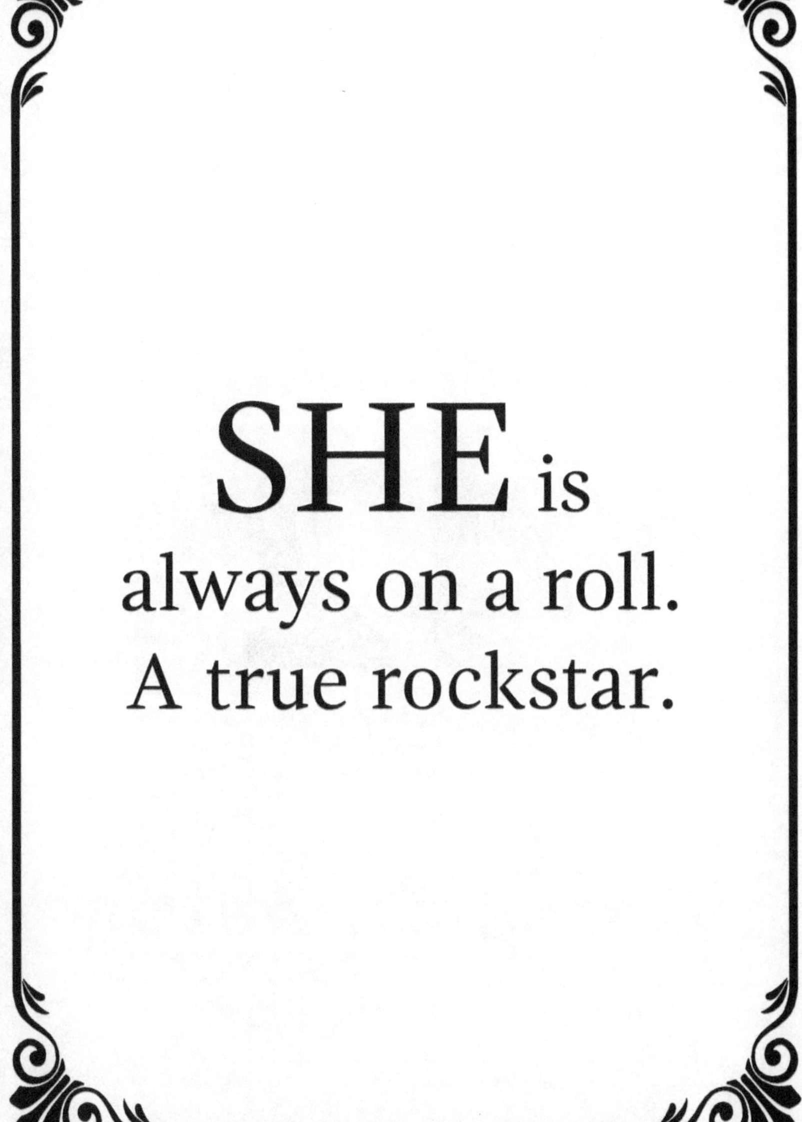

SHE is
always on a roll.
A true rockstar.

42

SHE likes things clean and tidy, shining and spotless.

SHE makes dreams comes true, hers as well as others.

44

SHE has a golden heart and loves her gold too. Enough to call her a *golden lady*?

45

SHE is
an epitome
of hard work,
smart work and
teamwork. All at
the same time.

46

SHE is that "behind every successful man, there is a woman".

47

SHE speaks such that it has more weightage than the gravity of the earth.

48

SHE is beautifully experiencing motherhood 2.0 with her grandchildren and what a joy it is to watch them together!

49

SHE is a perfect example of "who rule the world? - women".

50

SHE is the queen of her own castle.

51

SHE is a tigress when it comes to fiercely protecting her cubs from the herd.

52

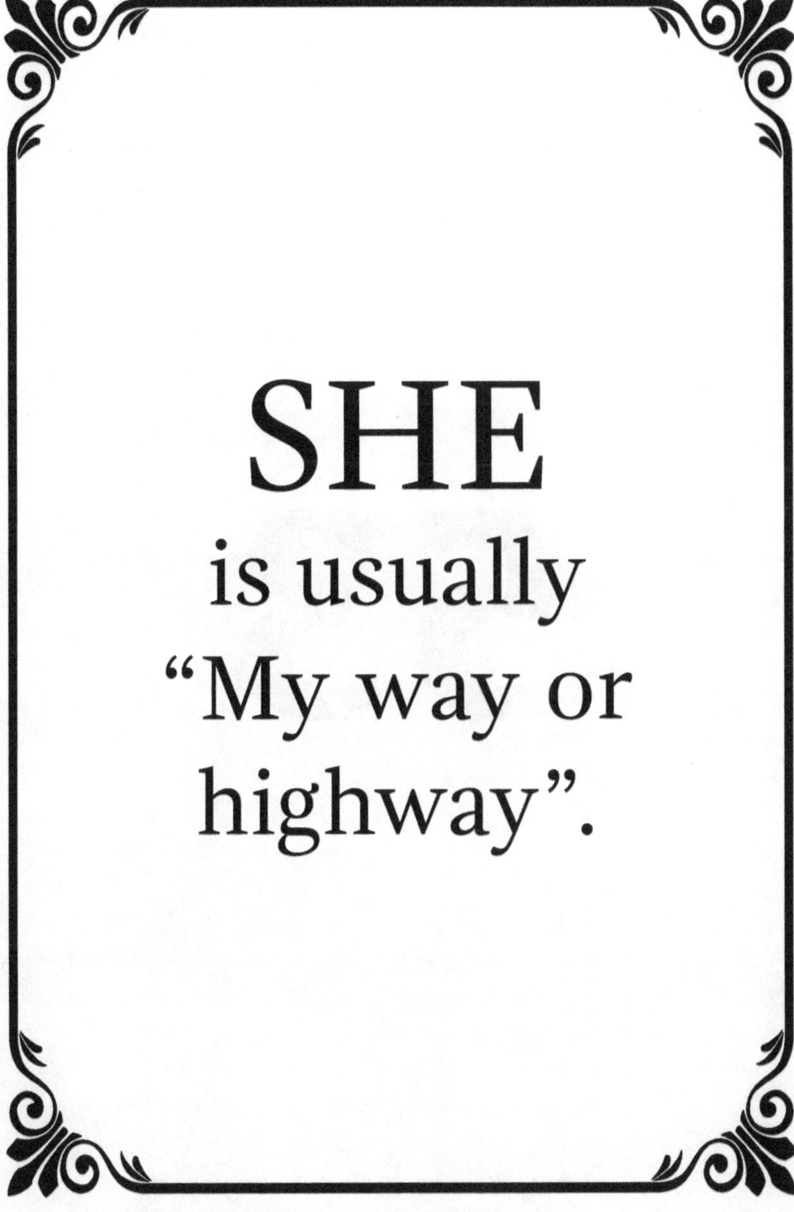

SHE
is usually
"My way or
highway".

53

SHE has built an empire all by herself...a true rags-to-riches story.

SHE makes the house come alive...the "*vaina vachakara*" of the house.

55

SHE is so powerful that her personality is her beauty.

56

SHE is young at heart and spirit, a "sweet 16".

57

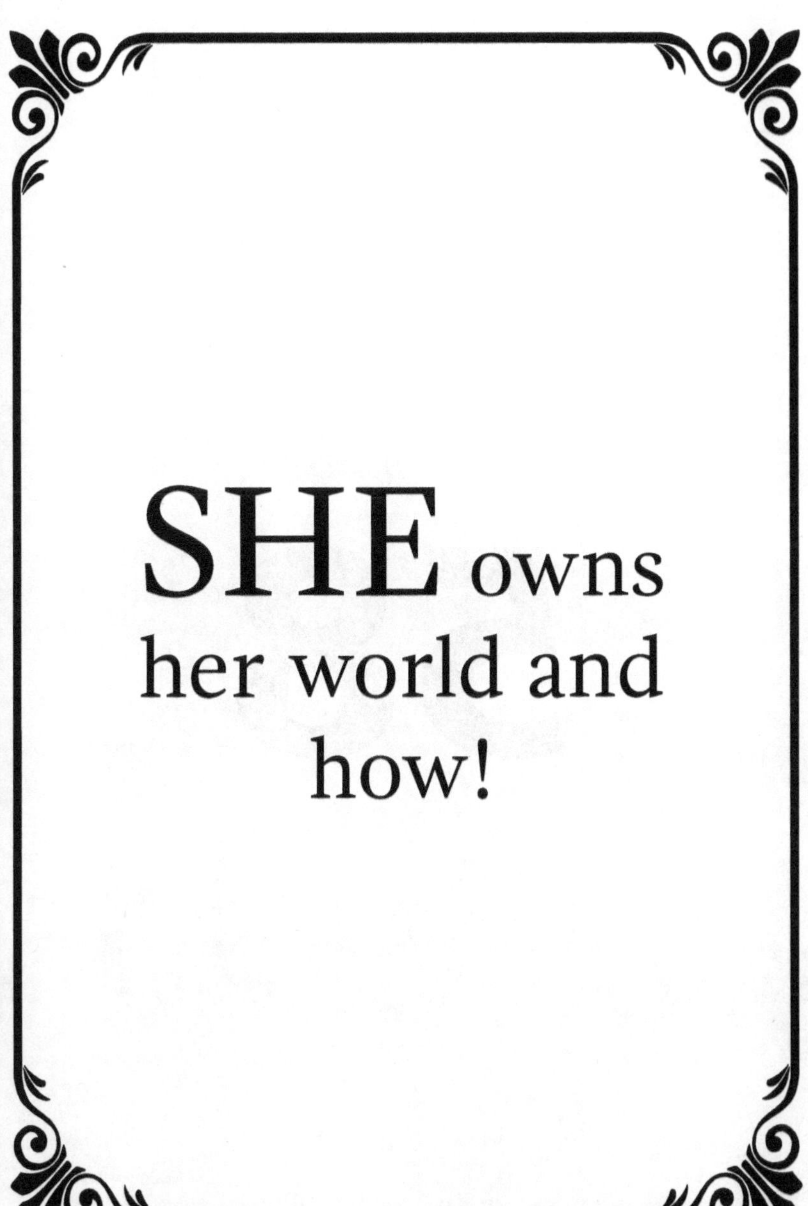

SHE owns her world and how!

58

SHE is the best thing that has ever happened to us and many others.

59

SHE is that woman, you would wonder "Is there anything she cannot do??"

60

SHE has led a glorious life and I hope her glorious journey lasts forever and ever!

Other book by the same author:

"Fun Intended"

A doctor by profession and an eternal romantic at heart. At the centre of her world are her witty hubby, mummy and pappa, her naughty little brother Tambi and her one-year-old pudding. Explore her world more to know her equation with autowalas, interesting patients, her gang of friends called 'family gang', eccentric guests, quirky staff and the great Indian aunts who have an opinion on everything! Sneak peek into childhood stories, MBBS days and mommy tales. Spicing up the scene are some funny instances with social media, cricket, periods, weddings, sex and shopping.

Welcome to her world! Fun totally intended!

ISBN 0000000000000

notionpress.com